If Words Could Kill

Yessika A. Garcia-Rosario

BookLeaf Publishing

Presentation by *BookLeaf Publishing*

Web: www.bookleafpub.com

E-mail: info@bookleafpub.com

ISBN: 978-93-95087-97-1

First edition 2022

To all the versions of myself that have died along the way.

Dakota and Jakari, my eternity

ACKNOWLEDGEMENTS

First and foremost, I would like to thank each and every one of you that took the time out to read my work. I have spent a significant amount of time trying to figure out the right words and placements to help portray my poetry, in the way I think is deserved. I hope this gives you something to hold on to forever.

I appreciate those family and friends who've encouraged me and loved me along the way.
I love you all wholeheartedly.
I would like to extend my gratitude to,
Jada Ramos for inspiring me in various ways with her sweet words, kind gestures, and for always giving me a shoulder to cry on. This would not have been possible if it wasn't for you.
Luz Gomez. My best friend, you have lived through most of these moments with me, and I don't know where I would be without you.
My siblings, Valerie Diaz-Rosario, Jorge Torres-Rosario, Sergio Garcia-Rosario and Yelissa Villa. I hold you all near and dear to my heart. I wouldn't be who I am today, if it wasn't for you all.

I cannot begin to express my appreciation and love for my mother, who has given me everything even if it meant that she had nothing.

No words could describe how lucky I am to have you. I love you.
To my aunts Jennyfer, Adriana, and Jade (and to whom you were before), I appreciate you forever. I have never felt alone because of you. I love you.

I am most grateful to Amber Shaw for believing in me enough to bring this opportunity up to my attention.
And lastly, Book Leaf Publishing who has given my work a new journey.

A book is merely nothing but everything. I leave my heart, pain, tears and love in these pages to you.

"Three things cannot be long hidden: the sun,
the moon, and the truth"
Gautama Buddha

CONTENT

November 14 17 1202 am

An I love you means nothing if it isn't from the
person you want to hear it from
An I miss you means nothing if it isn't from the
person you're missing
But just because the person you want doesn't
want you, doesn't mean you aren't worthy of
loving or living
It takes time and the right state of mind to get to
where the love you give out in return, is given
Make sure all grudges within are forgiven
To love yourself and care for yourself are things
that don't need permission
So do not let anyone else decide for you, how
things should be driven
Don't ignore the signs of toxic relations
If you hear something, try to really sit and listen
I know listening leads to thinking but to think is
to see
And if seeing is believing
Believe me when I say you're worth it
You're worth it,
An I love you means everything when you love
yourself

November 15 17 1101 pm

Defusing, defusing, defusing
The fusion we once had is now
Confusion, none of this is getting better just
more
Confusing, I feel like all of this is consuming
Time consuming for you
As for me I wish we had more chemistry
Chemistry, what we once had
But now it's something more like symmetry
We're the same in every possible way
But one,
The most important one,
Two peas in a pod, it's not what we are
We're more like black and white
Up and down
Left and right
But you know what they say, opposites attract
The fact is that we are more alike than we'd like
to believe
We need mystery not symmetry
But we can't bare to let each other go
Because the thought of us finding that same
symmetry in someone else, kills us
So we stay
Defusing, lets hope our relationship is defusing

February 10 18

If actions speak louder than words
then you've been screaming
But I'm so caught up in your daze,
I keep on dreaming
You tell me that you love me
But your eyes they've stopped gleaming
Although I have my doubts
I keep on believing
I'm so blinded by your love
I stop from seeing
You start to tell me that I'm the one who's
misleading
So I try to understand what I've done
while you keep creeping,
"Maybe I'm worrying to much"
"Maybe I'm tweaking"
Like nah, "he loves me, he can't be scheming"
So I keep ignoring the feeling
It's like I've cut myself and I keep ignoring the
bleeding
I stop assuming
I just watch and observe while you go do things
Tell me you'll be home at this time, won't come
Here come the excuses
"I was up all night with the boys, we were just
cruising"
It's like you can't control what you're doing
Playing this game with me and I continuously
keep losing
But as soon as you realize I've lost, you stop me
from moving

I try to say something but I'm muted
I just want to understand what I did to make you
do this
Time heals all wounds
but I'm still bruising
And although it sucks I know I got to push
through it
The day dreaming has turned lucid
I'm trying to wake up from this nightmare
but damn, I just can't do it

May 24 18

I'm beginning to think that I'm meant to sink,
that my breaths of air are destined to shrink
The pen I'm using to write my story is running
low on ink
in the middle of me sketching a picture of
something that will never exist
Trying to understand why life has so many
disastrous things
Why someone who's been married for several
years suddenly loses their ring
I understand that some people aren't meant to
act and sing,
so why do they tell us that practice makes
perfect?
If I practice enough will I feel like I'm worth it?
Do I deserve this?
Don't they tell us to "take a risk?"
If I risk it all will I reach my bliss?
Late night thoughts got me questioning things
The harder I try not to, the harder I think
I'm losing grip
It's hard to find happiness in a life of sin

June 09 18 1250 pm

If I fall in love again, I'll make sure not to rely
on it like some drug
No addiction
Something with little friction
Unless we're kissing
Can't overdose, if it ain't a prescription
Cause I ain't spending no extra time, money or
effort on something that does me no good
Never settling for less
The little engine that could
No more going over the edge for someone who
shouldn't but would
Need to find something I don't need to explain
cause it's already understood
I base things off of chemistry
But lately, people lie just to match energy
Different people, same lies
Repetitively
I'm willing to try something new
Receptively
Imagine getting what you give
Integrity
Ain't rushing anything, it just isn't worth it
Rushing won't ever make it perfect
But remember, there's footprints on the moon so
if I want more than the world, I think I deserve it

June 12 18 1000 pm — August 08 18 114 am

If you move on from me that's good to know
Just don't come back when there's nowhere else
to go
Either you want me, or you don't
A simple yes or no
I'm tired of being thought of when I let you go
If my love isn't enough then there's nothing else
for me to give
When you're left alone with no one else,
remember all the wrongs I was willing to forgive
How selfish you were to someone who has never
gave you a motive
I loved you through it all
I was always there to break the fall
I still catch myself reacting to them midnight
calls,
them midnight texts,
telling me you love me and want nothing but the
best
For us
But what am I to do when you pick lust over
trust?
Lust over love?
Enough is enough
My head and heart tell me two different things
Ones telling me yes
The other is telling me I'm more than this
I'm more than what you give to me,
I'm more than what I see

And if you can't see that after all these years,
then I guess it's finally time for me to leave

May 07 19 5 04 am −2 58 pm

My gut instinct about you was right
I didn't even think twice
I'm sorry you thought different just because I
was nice
You messed with everything around me,
to get me to notice you
You took the person I wanted and made them act
as if they hated me
You made them exchange me for loyalty
Something you know nothing about
You take to take and never give to give
You took me for you and never asked me what I
wanted to do
You manipulated the situation to benefit YOU
But what about me?
You see, you're heartless
Love at first sight?
I should've thought twice
But just as you messed with everything around
me, you messed with me
First my mind, then my heart
I couldn't tell truth from lies not even from the
start
Why do you lie?
You've begged me so many times for
forgiveness,
why do you cry?
I'm sorry for all the hurt you've been through,
but I've never known hurt until I met you
Sad? Yes
True? Ask anyone who knew me before you

I've never had to struggle with myself
But I
put my heart on my sleeve
Left my mind on the shelf
For you
But why
did I
do it to myself?
Because you made everything feel too good to
be true
and I believed you
That's exactly what it was, it was too good it
was NOT true,
for you.
For me, it was everything I've always wanted
until the lies started catching up
I left every time you messed up
But the face you put on after I did, made
everything tough
I started questioning myself
"Am I being too rough?"
My second mistake, the first was letting you in.
You took me back every time and that's why I
thought you loved me
But every time you took me back you loved me
a little less
I became a mess
I had all these thoughts in my head, all this
devotion in my heart
No one to blame but myself
That's what caused the stress
"Just go" I thought
"Just leave, it's best"
No.

My heart felt more
"There are those worth fighting for"
And I thought you were one.
Wrong.
All you wanted to do was have fun
You still told me you loved me, you still kept me around and I stayed because I loved you and I hated seeing you down
Have you ever felt the sensation you feel right before you drown?
That's how I felt when I saw you
That's how I felt when I derailed more lies
A thousand tries
A million fights
None were your fault until you seen me trying to move on
That's when I was asked to stay
because if I didn't "I never loved you"
Because if I didn't "It was never true"
"Things will be different" but you never intended to change
You stayed the same
I admit to my faults, I've apologized
How I've agonized
Maybe it would be easier if we didn't have kids
Going half on two babies was the best thing I've ever did
With you.
I will never forget
that situation with you and another who
But I won't explain because I am not Dr. Seuss
And the pain that I felt is something I don't want to reminisce on, not even for you.
This is how I'm grieving a life that still lives on

This is how I'm leaving a love that still goes on
Day by day
Line by line
I'm sorry I loved you before it was your time

November 22 18 304 am — July 07 19 818 pm

I am thankful for everything that I've been given
If it's in the past, then it's forgiven
If you dwell on things that have brought you pain,
then you're not living.
Eyes ahead
Focus
Look at your future, it should be vivid.
Do not doubt yourself
Do not be timid.
There's a life after death
So do not beat yourself down if this life isn't the best
You'll reach failure before reaching success.
And note: being successful isn't about the riches,
it's about reaching true happiness within
Being able to be alone and still feel those tummy kisses
Loving you
Before loving them too
Being happy with what you see
Knowing when enough is enough
Even if it seems tough
Knowing who you are and who you want to be
Setting goals that are possible to reach
Knowing the difference between dreams and reality
Letting go when it's time to leave

Realizing that it isn't impossible to find inner
peace
if you just believe
In YOU

April 06 19 134 am — May 23 19 111 am

All is forgiven
All is well
But them late night thoughts make it hard to tell
if I'm angry or upset
if I'm over it just yet
I live in a life of stress
Wondering why it's so hard for me to be my best
Why I always think of myself as less
Why it's always easier for me to say yes
instead of no
All is forgiven
All is well
But those late night tears make it hard to tell
if I'm sad it's gone or happy it ended
if anyone's noticed that I've pretended
To be happy
Happy.
I want to be happy
And it starts with me
All is forgiven
All is well

June 18 19 1211 am — July 09 19 1136 pm

I write to let my feelings go
To let my feelings flow
To let my feelings ask me what they wanna know
About any and everything
About who, what, where, when, why
About the things I deny
The things I try to hide
About all the things people have told me that were lies
Sometimes I try
to forget
To stop writing, close my eyes and get some rest
But you see that's when the stress eats me up the most
That's when my body is no longer my host,
when I lose control
And all these different scenarios put on a show
Trying to push these thoughts out of my head because they're making it hard for me to see,
I mean to hear,
I mean to think
It's like when you start drinking and before you know it, you've already reached your sixth drink
It becomes a habit
Sooner or later you can't stop yourself from grabbing it
It's your way of escaping
Your way of making sense of it all

You know it'll be there for you even when you
fall
It'll never judge you,
It'll never give up on you,
It'll be there for you as long as you need
Through all the good and bad times it's helped
you breathe
And you know for a fact it won't ever leave

August 04 19 150 am

Just because my heart hurts, doesn't make it right
It's flight or fight
And I think I'm flying; I gave out my heart and
it felt like I was dying
Everyday I'm trying to forgive and forget
Everyday I'm trying not to live with regret
I left
I had to leave
I was seeing a world of color
But you were seeing a green screen
I finally realized it wasn't me
It wasn't you
It was us
We put up these walls and neglected our trust
When things got rough,
we made them rougher
Just to see which one of us was tougher
No matter how much I loved you
I now know I am not your lover
I'm not the one,
it's not me
I just hope when you find her you won't put her
through what you did to me
I hope she understands you aren't easy to love
but you aren't easy to leave
I hope she understands that you need her like
you needed me
That there are wounds I left open for her to see
And somethings she won't understand but I hope
she doesn't make it bigger than what it seems

January 14 20 1224 am — 1246 am

Do you know that feeling?
The feeling you get when you don't know what
to feel
That feeling that lingers on your breath after
you've cried for hours
That feeling you get when everything possible
seems impossible,
like eating or sleeping
The feeling you get when you know you could
be doing more but your bed says different
That feeling you get when someone asks you
how you're doing, and you say okay even if
you're not
That feeling you get when what's in your head
and what's in your heart don't line up
That feeling when you feel so much but aren't
sure why you feel the way you feel
That feeling
Do you know it?

September 11 20 1022 am

To those who've hurt me
but didn't know,
I forgive you,
I let it go.
To those who've hurt me
and didn't care,
I hope you get what you deserve.
I hope you find love.
I hope you find the love you need to make you
feel
and I hope all the sins you've revealed, heal.
To those who've hurt me,
you might not have shattered my heart
but you've shifted my mind.
If thoughts could speak,
you would've shifted my language.
If emotions were actions,
I would've caused World War III.
But I chose me.
I chose sanity.
I silenced my pain and expanded my mind,
you see, the pen will always be mightier than the
sword.
To those who've hurt me,
I will be okay.

March 30 21 248 pm

For sorrow I've known like a brother
through empty rooms and empty promises
long sighs and soft cries
For loneliness I've known like a sister
the ability to see, hear, touch but not feel
Does it make one weak or stronger?
For regret I've known like a sinner
gun cocked, the finger squeezes the trigger
For love I've known like a father,
always present but never there
For anger I've known like a mother
and I've known her my whole life

November 11 21 1235 am — 559 am

I wear my heart on my sleeve,
so, I try my best to cover it up
But you lay your head on my chest
and you hear everything that I've been through
It's pointless for me to deny
the way you make me feel
I still try to hide
Behind tough phrases and faces
I still try to lie
and say I'm fine
Hoping you don't recognize the voice of a liar
You whisper pretty things to me,
sure, compliments are nice but I'm talking words
of affirmation
Words of moral support and motivation
This is too good to be true
or is this something way overdue?
Call me a fool if you want but this time feels
different
Or is this like every other time I made a hasty
decision?

December 10 21

How can I
decide
deny
define
that I am broken?
How can I say that I am helpless?
When the only guidance I need is from myself
"Self"
What do I identify as?
What do I want?
Why is it so hard to ignore my thoughts and
follow my heart?
How am I living this life for myself?
When every decision I make effects everyone
else
It's a chain reaction
If I react, I might trigger someone's anxiety
I might say something wrong
I might not say enough
All of a sudden, it's my fault
All of a sudden, I ignored red flags
that were never there
to begin with
If I don't react, get this
I get labeled cold hearted
Or a bitch
I get labeled weird
I get labeled a liar
And just like that trauma burns throughout my
body like a fire
No matter how hot it is it still burns

and no matter how cold it gets, I'm still scarred
They tell us to live life in our truth
But what if the truth is, I don't want to be here
anymore?
Am I broken?

December 10 21 550 pm — February 11 22 957 pm

I have a passion in my heart that yearns for
mystery
It yearns for double dates
For crossword puzzles on a gloomy day
It yearns for attention
but just enough
For understanding and compassion
It yearns for unconditional love
even when my attitude tells you it doesn't
For sidewalk talks and midday naps
For your interpretation of success
of happiness
of hate
I want to hear your rendition of a song
while I laugh at every note that doesn't fit
I want to feel you thrust against my hips
as you lean in for a kiss
I have a passion in my heart that yearns for
intimacy,
but that of beyond physical touch
that of beyond physical love
I want to be that song you skip to,
after deliberately putting your playlist on shuffle
I have a passion in my heart that yearns for love
Real love, even it fades with the moments of
time

When a boy says he loves you
what he means is girl I'm tryna get some
but I know I can't if I don't hold those emotions
When a boy says he loves you
what he means is I want you to love me more
than you can fathom
I want you to want me to want you but I can't
because I might find someone I want
When a boy says he loves you
he won't just say it
he will caress you with it
shove the words so far down your throat
you won't be able to breath without him
He will hold you like he holds in those tears
after a tragic event
but like those tears
he will neglect you
When a boy says he loves you
he thinks you're supposed to say it back
love him back
love him even if he stabs you in the back
love him and never look back
love him even when he stops loving you back
When a boy says he loves you
what he means is I got commitment issues
but to break the ice before I break you
I will say I love you
When a boy says he loves you
shit maybe he loves you

but make sure you're willing to love him
through it all
before you say it back

April 29 22 900 pm — 903 pm

I give to you my heart
Whole
Folded
Open
Woven into one
dissected
Chewed up
written on
And left to rot until there's none.

May 07 19 508 am —523 am

I thought so many harsh things when I was
pregnant with you
How 1+1 had to equal 2
And if it equaled 3 there was something wrong
with me
How I had to minus the problem
But there was no problem at all
There was something wrong with me
Something wrong with my head
These bad ideas occurred where I dimmed your
light
But why did I think that was right
Why did I think it was okay to make a decision
for you when you had no life?
It was that same light that brought me out of my
darkness
Imagine if I would've dimmed the light
I would've been consumed and given up the
fight
Because dimming the light wouldn't have
stopped the darkness from coming through
It would've made it darker
and I would've lost myself too
I thank you each and every day for coming to
me instead of me coming to you
You came for me when I needed you
You helped me see with a clearer view
You helped me understand why 1+1 was never 2
I love you

September 12 19 450 am — September 17 19 202 am

My first heartbreak was at eight years old
I use to pray, everyday
I use to ask for his whereabouts, if he was safe,
if I could see him one last time,
if I could remember him more than what I did
He got ripped away from my life,
ripped away from my head
but he was always in my heart
Someone recently asked me if I believe the
saying "Everything happens for a reason"
And I said I do,
I do because even if it isn't for your reasons, it
may be for someone else's
My dad was an alcoholic
I use to pray, every day
I'd ask God to make him stop
He was abusive
God listened to me and he made it stop
I promised myself I'd never love another man
again
At twelve years old I fell in love
I asked God what I did to deserve it
I denied it every day until I didn't
The beginning of my second heart ache
After my fourteenth birthday I stopped praying
and after my fifteenth I stopped believing
When I was sixteen years old, I got pregnant
I asked God what I did to deserve it

I asked God if there was a place in heaven for
my baby
When I was seventeen years old, I gave birth to
the love of my life
I asked the universe what I did to deserve her
I love her the way I wish my dad could've loved
me

ABOUT THE AUTHOR

Raised in the city of Central Falls, Rhode Island, Yessika is the sole parent of two children. She did not start composing poetry until late 2017. Although Yessika has always been intrigued and appreciative of spoken word, music, and literature, she did not anticipate taking part in its impact. Yessika frequently publishes her work online to share with others. With this being her first published book, she hopes to inspire those who feel purposeless and uncertain of what they are meant to be. "Follow your heart and never look back."